The Scriptural Rosary

Featuring the Good News Translation

Edited by
REV. VICTOR HOAGLAND, C.P.

Illustrated by
WILLIAM LUBEROFF

Regina Press
New York

D1416060

Nihil Obstat:	Reverend Robert O. Morrissey, J.C.D.
	Censor librorum
	December 6, 2002
Imprimatur:	Most Reverend William Murphy
	Bishop of Rockville Centre
	December 8, 2002

THE REGINA PRESS
10 Hub Drive
Melville, New York

Scripture quotations taken from GOOD NEWS TRANSLATION WITH DUETEROCANONCALS/APOCRYPHA, SECOND EDITION, Copyright © 1992 by American Bible Society, Used by permission. "Permission requests must be directed to, and approved in writing by, The Zondervan Corporation, 5300 Patterson Avenue, S.E., Grand Rapids, Michigan, 49530, USA."

ISBN# 0-88271-177-6

Printed in Hong Kong.

The Rosary

"To recite the rosary is nothing other than to contemplate the face of Christ with Mary."

Pope John Paul II

In his letter "Rosarium Virginis Mariae"(October 16, 2002) Pope John Paul II expressed his esteem for a method of praying that has nourished the faith of generations of Christians. The pope called on Catholics – and other Christians as well – to pray the rosary and enter "the school of Mary," who knew Jesus Christ so well as his mother and who was his closest disciple.

Though it is not mandatory, the pope also suggested that five mysteries be added to the traditional fifteen. He called them "Luminous Mysteries," or the Mysteries of Light, which include the mysteries of Christ's public ministry between his Baptism and his Passion. While leaving the use of these mysteries "to the freedom of individuals and communities," Pope John Paul suggested that they could help make the prayer more deeply centered in the life of Christ.

This book includes the Luminous Mysteries, taken from a period of Jesus' life when he revealed himself as "the Light of the world," and incorporates them into the fifteen traditional mysteries.

The Rosary and the Scriptures

Pope John Paul II also recommended the use of scriptural verses to accompany each mystery of the rosary in order to deepen the scriptural dimension of this prayer. This book offers scriptural verses as well as short meditations before each mystery.

The Rosary: Where Did It Come From?

Praying the rosary well is more important than knowing its history, yet knowing the origins of the prayer can teach us much about it.

The beginnings of the rosary are found in the early Christian practice of reciting the 150 psalms from the bible, either daily or weekly, as a way of prayer. Those unable to recite the psalms began to recite 150 payers, mainly the Our Father, 150 times, often using beads to count the prayers. By medieval times the custom of saying "Paternoster" beads (the Latin for Our Father) was common in many countries of Europe. While saying the prayers it was customary to meditate on the mysteries of the life of Jesus, from his birth to his resurrection.

The rosary in its present form arose in late medieval Christianity when Mary, the Mother of Jesus, was seen as a guide to the mysteries of her Son. A decade of prayers called the Hail Mary was preceded

6.
Meditate on 3rd Mystery, saying the "Our Father," ten "Hail Marys" and the "Glory Be."

7.
Meditate on 4th Mystery, saying the "Our Father," ten "Hail Marys" and the "Glory Be."

5.
Meditate on 2nd Mystery, saying the "Our Father," ten "Hail Marys" and the "Glory Be."

8.
Meditate on 5th Mystery, saying the "Our Father," ten "Hail Marys" and the "Glory Be."

4.
Meditate on 1st Mystery, saying the "Our Father," ten "Hail Marys" and the "Glory Be."

9.
Concluding prayer, "Hail Holy Queen"

3.
Say three "Hail Marys" and the "Glory Be."

2.
Say the "Our Father".

1.
Make the Sign of the Cross, say the Apostles' Creed.

by the Our Father. Meditation on the mysteries of Christ remained at the heart of the prayer.

Through the centuries, saints like St. Dominic, many of the popes, as well as countless ordinary Christians have found the rosary to be a school of prayer and a source of spiritual blessing. It is both simple and profound. Not beyond anyone's reach, its repeated words bring peace to the soul. And the mysteries of Jesus that it recalls are also meant to be repeated on our own. We ask to "imitate what they contain and obtain what they promise, through Christ our Lord."

Why We Pray the Rosary

The rosary is a special way of praying. As we recite the prayers of the rosary, we think about certain stories in the lives of Jesus and Mary.

These stories are called "mysteries". A mystery is a story about God and God's life in another person. We use rosary beads to help us keep count of the prayers and the mysteries.

How to Pray the Rosary

The complete rosary consists of twenty decades, but it is further divided into four distinct parts, the Joyful, the Luminous, the Sorrowful, and the Glorious Mysteries, each containing five decades.

To say the rosary, begin by making the sign of the cross and saying the Apostles' Creed on the crucifix, one Our Father on the first bead, three Hail Marys on the next three beads, and then a Glory Be to the Father. When this is finished, meditate upon the first mystery, say an Our Father, ten Hail Marys, and one Glory Be to the Father. The first decade is now completed, and to finish the rosary proceed in the same manner until all five decades have been said. When this is done, say one Hail Holy Queen.

As a prayer of faith, the rosary usually begins with two basic summaries of faith: the Sign of the Cross and the Creed. These prayers invite us to believe in God, the Father, the Son, and Holy Spirit, and to remember God's plan of salvation proclaimed in the scriptures.

The rosary is made up of decades of prayers. A decade of the rosary consists of an Our Father prayed before ten Hail Marys. At the end of a decade the prayer "Glory be to the Father, and to the Son, and to the Holy Spirit" is said. Most rosaries have five decades of beads.

The Mysteries of the Rosary

The rosary tells the story of Jesus in four parts. These parts are called mysteries. While praying the rosary, you may meditate on the mysteries of Jesus' life and resurrection. Twenty mysteries are presently associated with the rosary.

The Joyful Mysteries are:
Mondays and Saturdays

† **The Annunciation**

The Angel Gabriel tells Mary that she is to be the Mother of God.

† **The Visitation**

The Blessed Virgin pays a visit to her cousin Elizabeth.

† **The Birth of Jesus**

The Infant Jesus is born in a stable at Bethlehem.

† **The Presentation of the Child Jesus in the Temple**

The Blessed Virgin presents the Child Jesus to Simeon in the Temple.

† **The Finding of the Child Jesus in the Temple**

Jesus is lost for three days, and the Blessed Mother finds Him in the Temple.

The Luminous Mysteries are:
Thursdays

† **The Baptism of Jesus**

Jesus is baptized in the Jordan River by John the Baptist.

† **The Wedding at Cana**

Jesus attends a wedding at Cana in Galilee, where he turns water into wine.

✝ **The Proclamation of the Kingdom of God**
Jesus goes through the towns and cities of his
own country proclaiming God's Kingdom
and helping the poor.

✝ **The Transfiguration**
Jesus leads his friends up a high mountain,
where they see him shining in glorious light.

✝ **The Institution of the Holy Eucharist**
At supper with his friends before he dies,
Jesus gives himself to them in bread and wine.

The Sorrowful Mysteries are:
Tuesdays and Fridays

✝ **The Agony of Jesus in the Garden**
Jesus prays in the Garden of Olives and drops of
blood break through His skin.

✝ **The Scourging at the Pillar**
Jesus is tied to a pillar and cruelly
beaten with whips.

✝ **The Crowning with Thorns**
A crown of thorns is placed upon Jesus' head.

✝ **The Carrying of the Cross**
Jesus is made to carry His cross to Calvary.

✝ **The Crucifixion**
Jesus is nailed to the cross, and dies for our sins.

The Glorious Mysteries are:
Wednesdays and Saturdays

✝ **The Resurrection of Jesus from the Dead**
Jesus rises from the dead, three days
after His death.

✝ **The Ascension of Jesus into Heaven**
Forty days after His death,
Jesus ascends into heaven.

✝ **The Descent of the Holy Spirit**
Ten days after the Ascension, the Holy Spirit
comes to the apostles and the Blessed Mother in
the form of fiery tongues.

✝ **The Assumption of Mary into Heaven**
The Blessed Virgin is assumed into heaven.

✝ **The Crowning of Mary Queen of
Heaven and Earth**
The Blessed Virgin is crowned Queen
of Heaven and Earth by Jesus, her Son.

Prayers of the Rosary

The Sign of the Cross

In the name of the Father, ✝ and of the Son, and of the Holy Spirit. Amen.

The Apostles' Creed

I believe in God, the Father Almighty, Creator of heaven and earth; and in Jesus Christ, his only Son, our Lord, who was conceived by the Holy Spirit; born of the Virgin Mary, suffered under Pontius Pilate, was crucified, died and was buried. He descended into hell; the third day he rose again from the dead; he ascended into heaven, and is seated at the right hand of God the Father; from thence he shall come to judge the living and the dead. I believe in the Holy Spirit, the Holy Catholic Church, the communion of saints, the forgiveness of sins, the resurrection of the body, and life everlasting. Amen.

The Hail Mary

Hail Mary, full of grace, the Lord is with you; blessed are you among women, and blessed is the fruit of your womb, Jesus. Holy Mary, Mother of God, pray for us sinners, now and at the hour our death. Amen.

The Our Father

Our Father who art in heaven, hallowed be thy name; thy kingdom come; thy will be done on earth as it is in heaven. Give us this day our daily bread; and forgive us our trespasses as we forgive those who trespass against us. And lead us not into temptation; but deliver us from evil. Amen.

The Hail, Holy Queen

Hail, holy Queen, Mother of Mercy! Our life, our sweetness, and our hope! To thee do we cry, poor banished children of Eve; to thee do we send up our sighs, mourning and weeping in this valley of tears. Turn, then, most gracious advocate, thine eyes of mercy toward us; and after this our exile show unto us the blessed fruit of thy womb Jesus; O clement, O loving, O sweet Virgin Mary.

V. Pray for us, O holy Mother of God.

R. That we may be made worthy

of the promises of Christ.

Glory Be to the Father

Glory be to the Father, and to the Son, and to the Holy Spirit; as it was in the beginning, is now, and ever shall be, world without end. Amen.

The Joyful Mysteries of the Rosary

THE FIRST JOYFUL MYSTERY
The Annunciation

Meditation

The angel Gabriel says to Mary that she is going to be the mother of Jesus. We imagine and remember how Mary was asked to be the Mother of God. She said "Yes" to God's special invitation, and the child Jesus began to live and grow inside her body. Although she was a little bit frightened, Mary trusted God's request. She prayed that she would be a good mother.

📖 **Our Father** 📖

...God sent the angel Gabriel to a town in Galilee named Nazareth.

Luke 1.26

✝ **Hail Mary** ✝

He had a message for a young woman promised in marriage to a man named Joseph, who was a descendant of King David. Her name was Mary.

Luke 1.27

✝ **Hail Mary** ✝

The angel came to her and said, "Peace be with you!
The Lord is with you and has greatly blessed you!"

Luke 1.28

✝ Hail Mary ✝

Mary was deeply troubled by the angel's message,
and she wondered what his words meant.

Luke 1.29

✝ Hail Mary ✝

The angel said to her, "Don't be afraid, Mary; God has
been gracious to you. You will become pregnant and
give birth to a son, and you will name him Jesus."

Luke 1.30,31

✝ Hail Mary ✝

Mary said to the angel, "I am a virgin.
How, then, can this be?"

Luke 1.34

✝ Hail Mary ✝

The angel answered, "The Holy Spirit will come on
you, and God's power will rest upon you. For this
reason the holy child will be called the Son of God."

Luke 1.35

✝ Hail Mary ✝

"Remember your relative Elizabeth. It is said that she cannot have children, but she herself is now six months pregnant, even though she is very old."

Luke 1.36

✝ **Hail Mary** ✝

"For there is nothing that God cannot do."

Luke 1.37

✝ **Hail Mary** ✝

"I am the Lord's servant," said Mary; "may it happen to me as you have said." And the angel left her.

Luke 1.36

✝ **Hail Mary** ✝

Glory Be

THE SECOND JOYFUL MYSTERY
The Visitation

Meditation

Mary visits her cousin Elizabeth to tell her how happy she is that she is going to have a baby. Mary's Son would be Jesus, our Savior, and Elizabeth's son would be John, who would later become "the Baptist." John the Baptist would preach about the coming of the Savior.

📖 Our Father 📖

Soon afterwards Mary got ready and hurried off to a town in the hill country of Judea.

Luke 1.39

✝ Hail Mary ✝

She went into Zechariah's house and greeted Elizabeth.

Luke 1.40

✝ Hail Mary ✝

When Elizabeth heard Mary's greeting, the baby moved within her.

Luke 1.41

✝ Hail Mary ✝

Elizabeth was filled with the Holy Spirit and said in a loud voice, "You are the most blessed of all women,"
Luke 1.42

✝ **Hail Mary** ✝

"and blessed is the child you will bear!"
Luke 1.42

✝ **Hail Mary** ✝

"Why should this great thing happen to me, that my Lord's mother comes to visit me?"
Luke 1.43

✝ **Hail Mary** ✝

"For as soon as I heard your greeting, the baby within me jumped with gladness."
Luke 1.44

✝ **Hail Mary** ✝

"How happy you are to believe that the Lord's message to you will come true!"
Luke 1.45

✝ **Hail Mary** ✝

Mary said, "My heart praises the Lord; my soul is glad because of God my Savior."

Luke 1.46,47

✝ **Hail Mary** ✝

"For he has remembered me, his lowly servant! From now one all people will call me happy."

Luke 1.48

✝ **Hail Mary** ✝

Glory Be

THE THIRD JOYFUL MYSTERY
The Birth of Jesus

Meditation

It is easy to imagine the scene of Jesus' birth in a stable at Bethlehem. Mary and her husband, Joseph, lovingly welcome Jesus into their lives. They dream of the wonderful things they will show him, and they promise to care for him.

📖 Our Father 📖

Joseph went from the town of Nazareth in Galilee to the town of Bethlehem in Judea, the birthplace of Kind David. Joseph went there because he was a descendant of David. He went to register with Mary, who was promised in marriage to him.

Luke 2.4

✝ Hail Mary ✝

She was pregnant, and while they were in Bethlehem, the time came for her to have her baby.

Luke 2.6

✝ Hail Mary ✝

She gave birth to her first-born son, wrapped in cloths and laid him in a manger–there was no room for them to stay in the inn.

Luke 2.7

✝ **Hail Mary** ✝

There were some shepherds in that part of the country who were spending the night in the fields, taking care of their flocks.

Luke 2.8

✝ **Hail Mary** ✝

An angel of the Lord appeared to them, and the glory of the Lord shone over them. They were terribly afraid.

Luke 2.9

✝ **Hail Mary** ✝

But the angel said to them, "Don't be afraid! I am here with good news for you, which will bring great joy to all the people. This very day in David's town your Savior was born–Christ the Lord."

Luke 2.10,12

✝ **Hail Mary** ✝

Suddenly a great army of heaven's angels appeared with the angel, singing praises to God: "Glory to God in highest heaven, and peace on earth to those with whom he is pleased!"

Luke 2.13,14

✝ **Hail Mary** ✝

So they hurried off and found Mary and Joseph and saw the baby lying in the manger.

Luke 2.16

✝ **Hail Mary** ✝

When the shepherds saw him, they told them what the angel had said about the child. All who heard it were amazed at what the shepherds said.

Luke 2.17,18

✝ **Hail Mary** ✝

Mary remembered all these things and thought deeply about them.

Luke 2.19

✝ **Hail Mary** ✝

Glory Be

THE FOURTH JOYFUL MYSTERY
The Presentation of the Child Jesus in the Temple

Meditation

We picture Mary and Joseph bringing their infant son to the Temple. Here they thank God for their baby and promise to love and cherish him. As good Jewish parents, they offer their child to God. They also promise to teach him about God, who cares for us all.

📖 Our Father 📖

A week later, when the time came for the baby to be circumcised, he was named Jesus, the name which the angel had given him before he was conceived.
Luke 2.21

✝ Hail Mary ✝

The time came for Joseph and Mary to perform the ceremony of purification, as the Law of Moses commanded. So they took the child to Jerusalem to present him to the Lord.
Luke 2.22

✝ Hail Mary ✝

At that time there was a man named Simeon living in Jerusalem. He was a good, God-fearing man and was waiting for Israel to be saved. The holy Spirit was with him.
Luke 2.25,26

✝ **Hail Mary** ✝

Led by the Spirit, Simeon went into the Temple. When the parents brought the child Jesus into the Temple to do what the Law required, Simeon took the child in his arms and gave thanks to God.
Luke 2.27,28

✝ **Hail Mary** ✝

"Now, Lord, you have kept your promise, and you may let your servant go in peace."
Luke 2.29

✝ **Hail Mary** ✝

"With my own eyes I have seen your salvation, which you have prepared in the presence of all peoples."
Luke 2.31

✝ **Hail Mary** ✝

"A light to reveal your will to the Gentiles and bring glory to your people Israel."

Luke 2.32

✝ **Hail Mary** ✝

The child's father and mother were amazed at the things Simeon said about him.

Luke 2.32

✝ **Hail Mary** ✝

Simeon blessed them and said to Mary, his mother, "This child is chosen by God for the destruction and salvation of many in Israel. He will be a sign from God which many will speak against and so reveal their secret thoughts. And sorrow, like a sharp sword, will break your own heart."

Luke 2.34,35

✝ **Hail Mary** ✝

When Joseph and Mary had finished all that was required by the Law of the Lord, they returned to their hometown of Nazareth in Galilee. The child grew and became strong; he was full of wisdom, and God's blessing was upon him.

Luke 2.39,40

✝ **Hail Mary** ✝

Glory Be

THE FIFTH JOYFUL MYSTERY
The Finding of the Child Jesus in the Temple

Meditation

We recall another Temple scene when Jesus was a young boy. Jesus had stayed behind after the Temple service to talk to the priests and teachers. Mary and Joseph thought he was lost. When they found him, they were filled with joy and thanked God.

📖 Our Father 📖

Every year the parents of Jesus went to Jerusalem for the Passover festival. When Jesus was twelve years old, they went to the festival as usual.

Luke 2.41

✝ Hail Mary ✝

When the festival was over, they started back home, but the boy Jesus stayed in Jerusalem.

Luke 2.43

✝ Hail Mary ✝

*His parents did not know this; they thought he was
with the group, so they traveled a whole day
and then started looking for him among their
relatives and friends.*

Luke 2.44

† **Hail Mary** †

*They did not find him, so they went back to
Jerusalem looking for him.*

Luke 2.45

† **Hail Mary** †

*On the third day they found him in the Temple,
sitting with the Jewish teachers, listening to them and
asking questions.*

Luke 2.46

† **Hail Mary** †

*All who heard him were amazed at his intelligent
answers.*

Luke 1.47

† **Hail Mary** †

His parents were astonished when they saw him and his mother said to him, "Son, why have you done this to us? Your father and I have been terribly worried trying to find you."

Luke 2.48

✝ **Hail Mary** ✝

He answered them, "Why did you have to look for me? Didn't you know that I had to be in my Father's house?"

Luke 2.49

✝ **Hail Mary** ✝

But they did not understand his answer.

Luke 2.50

✝ **Hail Mary** ✝

So Jesus went back with them to Nazareth, where he was obedient to them. His mother treasured all these things in her heart. Jesus grew both in body and in wisdom, gaining favor with God and people.

Luke 2.51,52

✝ **Hail Mary** ✝

Glory Be

The Luminous Mysteries of the Rosary

THE FIRST LUMINOUS MYSTERY
The Baptism of Jesus

Meditation

Usually the story of Jesus begins with his birth in Bethlehem, but New Testament sources such as the Gospel of Mark begin his story with Jesus' Baptism. Jesus is God's only Son, but in Baptism his followers become children of God too. With no claim of our own, we are invited by him into God's family and we go in his name to bring goodness and healing to the world in which we live.

📖 Our Father 📖

John appeared in the desert, baptizing and preaching. "Turn away from your sins and be baptized," he told the people, "and God will forgive your sins."

Mark 1,4

✝ Hail Mary ✝

Not long afterward Jesus came from Nazareth in the province of Galilee and was baptized by John in the Jordan.

Mark 1,9

✝ Hail Mary ✝

As soon as Jesus came up out of the water,
he saw heaven opening
and the Spirit coming down on him like a dove.
Mark 1,10

✝ **Hail Mary** ✝

And a voice came from heaven,
"You are my own dear Son.
I am pleased with you."
Mark 1, 11

✝ **Hail Mary** ✝

"For God so loved the world so much that he gave
his only Son, so that everyone who believes in
him may not die but have eternal life."
John 3,16

✝ **Hail Mary** ✝

"Go throughout the whole world and preach the
gospel to all people. Whoever believes and is
baptized will be saved."
Mark 16,14

✝ **Hail Mary** ✝

Peter said to them, "Each one of you must turn away from your sins and be baptized in the name of Jesus Christ, so that your sins will be forgiven and you will receive God's gift, the Holy Spirit."

Acts 2,38

✝ **Hail Mary** ✝

"You were baptized into union with Christ, and now you are clothed, so to speak, with the life of Christ himself."

Galatians 3,27

✝ **Hail Mary** ✝

Those whom God had already chosen he also set apart to become like his Son, so that the Son may be the first among many believers.

Romans 8,29

✝ **Hail Mary** ✝

And those he called, he put right with himself, and he shared his glory with them.

Romans 8,30

✝ **Hail Mary** ✝

Glory Be

THE SECOND LUMINOUS MYSTERY
The Wedding at Cana in Galilee

Meditation

John's Gospel states that Jesus' public ministry began at a wedding feast that was heading for failure. The wine was running out, which meant the joy of the celebration would be dampened and the couple and their families would be embarrassed. By changing water into wine, Jesus saved the day. His first miracle brought joy to a group of men and women. In fact, this is why he came: to bring "great joy to all people."

📖 **Our Father** 📖

The Word became a human being and,
full of grace and truth, lived among us.
We saw his glory...

John 1, 14

✝ **Hail Mary** ✝

There was a wedding in the town of Cana in Galilee. Jesus' mother was there, and Jesus and his disciples had also been invited to the wedding.

John 2, 1-2

✝ **Hail Mary** ✝

When the wine had given out,
Jesus' mother said to him,
"They are out of wine."
"You must not tell me what to do,"
Jesus replied, "My time has not yet come."
John 2, 3-4

✝ **Hail Mary** ✝

Jesus' mother then told the servants,
"Do whatever he tells you."
John 2,5

✝ **Hail Mary** ✝

Jesus said to the servants
"Fill these jars with water."
They filled them to the brim,
and then he told them.
"Now draw some water out and take it to the
man in charge of the feast." They took him the
water, which now had turned into wine,
and he tasted it. He did not know where
this wine had come from.
John 2, 7-8

✝ **Hail Mary** ✝

He called the bridegroom and said to him,
"Everyone else serves the best wine first,
and after the guests have drunk a lot,
he serves the ordinary wine.
But you have kept the best wine until now."
                                                    John 2, 9-10

✝ Hail Mary ✝

Jesus performed this first miracle
in Cana in Galilee;
there he revealed his glory,
and his disciples believe in him.
                                                    John 2, 11

✝ Hail Mary ✝

No longer will you be called "Forsaken,"
"The Deserted Wife."
Or your land be called
"The Deserted Wife."
                                                    Isaiah 62,4

✝ Hail Mary ✝

Your new name will be
"God is Pleased with Her."
Your land will be called
"Happily Married,"
because the Lord is pleased with you
and will be like a husband to your land.
Isaiah 62,4

✝ **Hail Mary** ✝

Like a young man taking a virgin as his bride,
he who formed you will marry you.
As a groom is delighted with his bride,
so your God will delight in you.
Isaiah 62,5

✝ **Hail Mary** ✝

Glory Be

THE THIRD LUMINOUS MYSTERY
The Proclamation of the Kingdom of God

Meditation

After his Baptism in the Jordan, Jesus left the quiet safety of Nazareth to preach the Good News about the Kingdom. Crowds surrounded him as he went through Galilee, and he lifted their hearts with his words. "I am the resurrection and the life," he said, and he promised that those who believe in him would live, even though they will die.

📖 **Our Father** 📖

Jesus went all over Galilee, teaching in the synagogues, preaching the Good News about the Kingdom, and healing people who had all kinds of disease and sickness.

Mark 4, 23

✝ **Hail Mary** ✝

Then Jesus went home. Again such a large crowd gathered that Jesus and his disciples has no time to eat.

Luke 3,29

✝ **Hail Mary** ✝

When Jesus got out of the boat, he saw this large
crowd, and his heart was filled with pity for them,
because they were like sheep without a shepherd.
So he began to teach them many things.

Mark 6,34

✝ Hail Mary ✝

Then Jesus called the crowd and his disciples to
him. "If any of you want to come with me," he told
them, "you must forget yourself, carry your cross,
and follow me."

Mark 8,34

✝ Hail Mary ✝

Some people brought their babies to Jesus
for him to place his hands on them.
The disciples saw them and scolded them
for doing so, but Jesus called the children
to him and said,"let the children come to me
and do not stop them,
because the Kingdom of God belongs
to such as these."

Luke 18,15-16

✝ Hail Mary ✝

"I am the light of the world," he said.
"Whoever follows me will have
the light of life
and will never walk in darkness."

John 8,12

✝ **Hail Mary** ✝

"I am the good shepherd,
who is willing to die for the sheep."

John 10,11

✝ **Hail Mary** ✝

"I am the resurrection and the life.
Those who believe in me will live,
even though they die; and those who live and
believe in me will never die."

John11,25

✝ **Hail Mary** ✝

"I am among you as one who serves."

Luke 22,27

✝ **Hail Mary** ✝

"This, then, is what I command you:
love one another."

John 15,17

✝ **Hail Mary** ✝

Glory Be

THE FORTH LUMINOUS MYSTERY
The Transfiguration

Meditation

On the way to Jerusalem where he would be crucified, Jesus told his disciples of his coming sufferings and death. They were deeply saddened. Jesus was transfigured before them to show that God's glory endures. God's glory shines in the darkest places of our lives, if we hold them up to the light of faith. We are given intimations, brief encounters, transfigurations of a lesser kind, as we confront the mystery of suffering.

📖 Our Father 📖

Jesus took Peter, John, and James with him and went up a hill to pray. While he was praying, his face changed in appearance, and his clothes became dazzling white.

Luke 9,28-29

✝ Hail Mary ✝

Suddenly two men were there talking with him. They were Moses and Elijah, who appeared in heavenly glory and talked with Jesus about the way in which he would soon fulfill God's purpose by dying in Jerusalem.

Luke 9, 30-31

✝ Hail Mary ✝

Peter and his companions were sound asleep, but they woke up and saw Jesus' glory and the two men who were standing with him.

Luke 9, 32

† **Hail Mary** †

As the men were leaving Jesus, Peter said to him, "Master, how good it is that we are here. We will make three tents, one for you, one for Moses, and one for Elijah."

Luke 9,33

† **Hail Mary** †

While he was still speaking, a cloud appeared and covered them with its shadow; and the disciples were afraid as the cloud came over them.

Luke 9,34

† **Hail Mary** †

A voice said from the cloud, "This is my Son, whom I have chosen – listen to him!"

Luke 9,35

† **Hail Mary** †

*When the voice stopped, there was Jesus all alone.
The disciples kept quiet about all this and told no
one at the time anything they had seen.*

Luke 9,36

✝ Hail Mary ✝

*See how much the Father has loved us! His love is
so great that we are called God's children—and so,
in fact, we are.*

1John 3,1

✝ Hail Mary ✝

*We are God's children now, but it is not yet clear
what we shall become.*

1 John 3, 2

✝ Hail Mary ✝

*But we know that when Christ appears, we shall be
like him, because we shall see him as he really is.*

1 John 3,2

✝ Hail Mary ✝

Glory Be

THE FIFTH LUMINOUS MYSTERY
The Institution of the Holy Eucharist

Meditation

"I am the bread of life," Jesus told them. "Those who come to me will never be hungry; those who believe in me will never be thirsty." On the night before he died, Jesus gave his friends a lasting sign of his love for them. He gave them his body and his blood. For all the ages, he would be their bread of life. Through bread and wine, he gave them his body and blood.

📖 **Our Father** 📖

When it was evening, Jesus and the twelve disciples sat down to eat. During the meal Jesus said, "I tell you, one of you will betray me."
Matthew 26,20-21

✝ **Hail Mary** ✝

The disciples were very upset and began to ask him, one after the other, "Surely, Lord, you don't mean me?"
Matthew 26, 22

✝ **Hail Mary** ✝

Judas, the traitor, spoke up.
"Surely, Teacher, you don't mean me?"
he asked. Jesus answered, "So you say."
Matthew 26, 25

† **Hail Mary** †

While they were eating, Jesus took a piece of
bread, gave a prayer of thanks, broke it,
and gave it to his disciples.
"Take and eat it," he said, "this is my body."
Matthew 26, 26

† **Hail Mary** †

Then he took a cup, gave thanks to God,
and gave it to them.
"Drink it, all of you," he said;
"this is my blood,
which seals God's covenant,
my blood poured out for many
for the forgiveness of sins."
Matthew 26, 27

† **Hail Mary** †

"I am the bread of life," Jesus told them.
"Those who come to me
will never be hungry;
those who believe in me
will never be thirsty."

John 6, 35

✝ **Hail Mary** ✝

"Those who eat my flesh
and drink my blood have eternal life,
and I will raise them to life
on the last day."

John 6, 54

✝ **Hail Mary** ✝

"There are many rooms in my Father's house,
and I am going to prepare a place for you.
I will come back and take you to myself,
so that you will be where I am."

John 14, 3

✝ **Hail Mary** ✝

"Peace is what I leave with you;
it is my own peace that I give you.
Do not be worried and upset; do not be afraid."
John 14, 27

✝ **Hail Mary** ✝

"My commandment is this: love one another,
just as I love you. The greatest love you can
have for your friends is to give your life for them."
John 15, 12-13

✝ **Hail Mary** ✝

Glory Be

The Sorrowful Mysteries of the Rosary

THE FIRST SORROWFUL MYSTERY
The Agony of Jesus in the Garden

Meditation

Jesus knew that he had been betrayed by his own friend and rejected by the Jewish leaders. We can remember and imagine him talking to God. We picture him after his Last Supper going to pray in a garden. Knowing that his enemies are near, he is frightened. He does not want to die but finds the strength and courage to die to do so.

📖 **Our Father** 📖

They came to a place called Gethsemane,
and Jesus said to his disciples,
"Sit here while I pray."
He took Peter, James and John with him.
Mark 14.32,33

✝ **Hail Mary** ✝

Distress and anguish came over him
and he said to them,
"The sorrow in my heart is so great
that it almost crushes me. Stay here and keep watch."
Mark 14.34

✝ **Hail Mary** ✝

He went a little farther on, threw himself on the
ground, and prayed that, if possible, he might not
have to go through that time of suffering.
Mark 14.35

✝ **Hail Mary** ✝

"Father," he prayed, "my Father. All things are
possible for you. Take this cup of suffering away from
me. Yet not what I want, but what you want."
Mark 14.36

✝ **Hail Mary** ✝

Then he returned and found the three disciples
asleep. He said to Peter, "Simon, are you asleep?
Weren't you able to stay awake for even one hour?"
Mark 14.37

✝ **Hail Mary** ✝

And he said to them,
"Keep watch, and pray that
you will not fall into temptation.
The spirit is willing, but the flesh is weak."
Luke 14.38

✝ Hail Mary ✝

He went away once more and prayed,
saying the same words.
Then he came back to the disciples
and found them asleep;
they could not keep their eyes open.
Mark 14.39

✝ Hail Mary ✝

When he came back the third time, he said to them,
"Are you still sleeping and resting? Enough!
The hour has come!
Look the Son of Man is now
being handed over to the power of sinners."
Mark 14.41

✝ Hail Mary ✝

Jesus was still speaking when Judas, one of the twelve disciples, arrived. With him was a crowd armed with swords and clubs…

Mark 14.43

✝ **Hail Mary** ✝

As soon as Judas arrived, he went up to Jesus and said, "Teacher!" and kissed him. So they arrested Jesus and held him tight.

Mark 14.45

✝ **Hail Mary** ✝

Glory Be

THE SECOND SORROWFUL MYSTERY
The Scourging at the Pillar

Meditation

The Roman procurator, Pilate, orders Jesus to be whipped and beaten. We can picture the soldiers carrying out this command. Jesus was badly beaten by the soldiers. He silently accepted this sorrow and pain out of love for all humankind.

📖 **Our Father** 📖

Early in the morning Jesus was taken from Caiphas'
house to the governor's palace.

John 18.28

✝ **Hail Mary** ✝

Pilate went outside and asked,
"What do you accuse this man of?"

John 18.29

✝ **Hail Mary** ✝

Their answer was, "We would not have brought him to you if he had not committed a crime."

John 18.30

✝ **Hail Mary** ✝

Pilate went back into the palace and called Jesus. "Are you the king of the Jews?" he asked him.

John 18.33

✝ **Hail Mary** ✝

Jesus said, "My kingdom does not belong to this world."

John 18.36

✝ **Hail Mary** ✝

Pilate asked him, "Are you a king then?"

John 18.37

✝ **Hail Mary** ✝

Jesus answered, "You say I am a king. I was born and came into the world for this one purpose, to speak about the truth. Whoever belongs to the truth listens to me."

John 18.37

✝ **Hail Mary** ✝

*Then Pilate went outside to the people
and said to them, "I cannot find any reason to
condemn him. But according to the custom you have,
I always set free a prisoner for you
during the Passover. Do you want me to set free
for you the king of the Jews?"*

John 18.39

✝ Hail Mary ✝

*They answered him with a shout, "No, not him! We
want Barabbas!" (Barabbas was a bandit.)*

John 18.40

✝ Hail Mary ✝

Then Pilate took Jesus and had him whipped.

John 19.1

✝ Hail Mary ✝

Glory Be

THE THIRD SORROWFUL MYSTERY
The Crowning with Thorns

Meditation

We try to imagine now the hurt, bleeding Jesus being mocked. Jesus' hands are tied. A purple cloth is put on his shoulders and a crown of thorns put upon his head. The soldiers dance around him, spit at him, and mockingly call him king.

📖 **Our Father** 📖

The soldiers took Jesus inside the courtyard of the governor's palace and called together the rest of the company.

Mark 15.16

✝ **Hail Mary** ✝

The soldiers made a crown out of thorny branches and put it on his head.

John 19.2

✝ **Hail Mary** ✝

Then they put a purple robe on him and came to him and said, "Long live the King of the Jews!"
John 19.3

✝ **Hail Mary** ✝

And they went up and slapped him.
John 19.3

✝ **Hail Mary** ✝

Pilate went out once more and said to the crowd, "Look, I will bring him out here to let you see that I cannot find any reason to condemn him."
John 19.4

✝ **Hail Mary** ✝

So Jesus came out, wearing the crown of thorns and the purple robe.
John 19.5

✝ **Hail Mary** ✝

Pilate said to them, "Look, here is the man!
John 19.5

✝ **Hail Mary** ✝

*When the chief priests and Temple guards saw him,
they shouted, "Crucify him! Crucify him!"*

John 19.8

✝ **Hail Mary** ✝

*Pilate said to them, "You take him, then, and crucify
him. I find no reason to condemn him."*

John 19.6

✝ **Hail Mary** ✝

*But the crowd shouted back, "If you set him free,
that means that you are not the Emperor's friend.
Anyone who claims to be a king is a rebel
against the Emperor!"*

John 19.12

✝ **Hail Mary** ✝

Glory Be

THE FOURTH SORROWFUL MYSTERY
The Carrying of the Cross

Meditation

We picture Jesus carrying a rough, heavy wooden cross to Calvary, where he will die. Along the way, he meets his heartbroken mother and friends. They cry as sorrow fills them.

📖 Our Father 📖

Then all the disciples left him and ran away.

Matthew 26.56

✝ Hail Mary ✝

When they finished making fun of him, they took off the purple robe and put his own clothes back on him. Then they led him out to crucify him.

Mark 15.20

✝ Hail Mary ✝

The soldiers led Jesus away, and as they were going, they met a man from Cyrene who was coming into the city from the country.

Luke 23.26

✝ Hail Mary ✝

They seized him, put the cross on him, and made him carry it behind Jesus.

Luke 23.26

✝ **Hail Mary** ✝

A large crowd of people followed him; among them were some women who were weeping and wailing for him.

Luke 23.27

✝ **Hail Mary** ✝

Jesus turned to them and said, "Women of Jerusalem! Don't cry for me, but for yourselves and your children."

Luke 23.28

✝ **Hail Mary** ✝

Two other men, both of them criminals, were also led out to be put to death with Jesus.

Luke 28.32

✝ **Hail Mary** ✝

When they came to the place called "The Skull," they crucified Jesus there, and the two criminals, one on his right and the other on his left.

Luke 28.33

✝ **Hail Mary** ✝

There they tried to give him wine mixed with a drug called myrrh, but Jesus would not drink it.

Mark 15.23

✝ **Hail Mary** ✝

Jesus said, "Forgive them, Father! They don't know what they are doing."

Luke 28.34

✝ **Hail Mary** ✝

Glory Be

THE FIFTH SORROWFUL MYSTERY
The Crucifixion

Meditation

Imagine Jesus' mother now. Her child is hanging, nailed to a cross, and slowly dying. While he is dying, He asks God to forgive everyone, and then he gives his spirit over to God. Jesus showed his love for us by dying on a cross.

📖 **Our Father** 📖

It was nine o'clock in the morning when they crucified him. The notice of the accusation against him said: "The King of the Jews."
Mark 15.26

✝ **Hail Mary** ✝

People passing by shook their heads and hurled insults at Jesus: "Aha! You were going to tear down the Temple and build it back up in three days! Now come down from the cross and save yourself!"
Mark 15.29

✝ **Hail Mary** ✝

The soldiers also made fun of him; they came up to him and offered him cheap wine and said, "Save yourself if you are the king of the Jews."

Luke 23.36

✝ **Hail Mary** ✝

Standing close to Jesus' cross were his mother, his mother's sister, Mary the wife of Clophas, and Mary Magdalene.

John 19.25

✝ **Hail Mary** ✝

Jesus saw his mother and the disciple he loved standing there; so he said to his mother, "Here is your son."

John 19.26

✝ **Hail Mary** ✝

At noon the whole country was covered with darkness, which lasted for three hours. At three o'clock Jesus cried out with a loud shout, "Eloi, Eloi, lema sabachthani?" which means, "My God, my God, why did you abandon me?"

Mark 15.33,34

✝ **Hail Mary** ✝

Jesus cried out in a loud voice, "Father! In your hands I place my spirit!" He said this and died.

Luke 23.46

✝ **Hail Mary** ✝

It was toward evening when Joseph of Arimathea arrived. It was Preparation Day (that is, the day before the Sabbath), so Joseph went boldly into the presence of Pilate and asked for the body of Jesus.

Mark 15.42,43

✝ **Hail Mary** ✝

Joseph bought a linen sheet, took the body down, wrapped it in the sheet, and placed it in a tomb which had been dug out of solid rock.

Mark 15.46

✝ **Hail Mary** ✝

Then he rolled a large stone across the entrance to the tomb. Mary Magdalene and Mary the mother of Joseph were watching and saw where the body of Jesus was placed.

Mark 15.47

✝ **Hail Mary** ✝

Glory Be

The Glorious Mysteries of the Rosary

THE FIRST GLORIOUS MYSTERY
The Resurrection of Jesus from the Dead

Meditation

We picture Jesus coming forth from the tomb on Easter Sunday morning. Jesus' rising from the dead brings with it a promise of new life for us. Jesus has conquered death forever.

📖 **Our Father** 📖

Early on Sunday morning,
while it was still dark,
Mary Magdalene went to the tomb
and saw that the stone had been
taken away from the entrance.

John 20.1

✝ **Hail Mary** ✝

She went running to Simon Peter and the other disciple, whom Jesus loved, and told them, "They have taken the Lord from the tomb, and we don't know where they have put him."

John 20.2

† **Hail Mary** †

Mary stood crying outside the tomb. Then she turned around and saw Jesus standing there; but she did not know that it was Jesus. "Woman, why are you crying?" Jesus asked her. "Who is it you are looking for?"

John 20.14,15

† **Hail Mary** †

She thought he was the gardener, so she said to him, "If you took him away, sir, tell me where you have put him, and I will go and get him."

John 20.15

† **Hail Mary** †

Jesus said to her, "Mary!"

John 20.16

† **Hail Mary** †

She turned toward him and said in Hebrew,
"Rabboni!" (This means "Teacher")

John 20.16

✝ **Hail Mary** ✝

"Do not hold on to me," Jesus told her,
"because I have not yet gone back up to the Father.
But go to my brothers and tell them that I am
returning to him who is my Father and their Father,
my God and their God."

John 20.17

✝ **Hail Mary** ✝

So Mary Magdalene went and told the disciples that
she had seen the Lord and related to them what he
had told her.

John 20.18

✝ **Hail Mary** ✝

It was late that Sunday evening,
and the disciples were gathered together behind
locked doors, because they were afraid of the Jewish
authorities. Then Jesus came and stood among them.
"Peace be with you," he said.

John 20.19

✝ **Hail Mary** ✝

After saying this, he showed them his hands and his side. The disciples were filled with joy at seeing the Lord.

John 20.20

✝ **Hail Mary** ✝

Glory Be

THE SECOND GLORIOUS MYSTERY
The Ascension of Jesus into Heaven

Meditation

Imagine the friends and followers of Jesus as they watched him being lifted out of their sight. Jesus had taught them everything they needed to know, and he now returns to heaven.

📖 Our Father 📖

Before Jesus was taken up, he gave instructions by the power of the Holy Spirit to the men he had chosen as his apostles.

Acts 1.2

✝ Hail Mary ✝

For forty days after his death he appeared to them many times in ways that proved beyond doubt that he was alive.

Acts 1.3

✝ Hail Mary ✝

And when they came together, he gave them this order: "Do not leave Jerusalem, but wait for the gift I told you about, the gift my Father promised."

Acts 1.4

✝ **Hail Mary** ✝

Jesus said to them … "when the Holy Spirit comes upon you, you will be filled with power and you will be witnesses for me in Jerusalem, in all of Judea and Samaria, and to the ends of the earth."

Acts 1.8

✝ **Hail Mary** ✝

After saying this, he was taken up to heaven as they watched him, and a cloud hid him from their sight.

Acts 1.9

✝ **Hail Mary** ✝

They still had their eyes fixed on the sky as he went away, when two men dressed in white suddenly stood beside them and said,"Galileans, why are you standing looking up at the sky?"

Acts 1.10,11

✝ **Hail Mary** ✝

Then the apostles went back to Jerusalem from the Mount of Olives, which is about a mile away from the city.

Acts 1.12

✝ Hail Mary ✝

They gathered frequently to pray as a group, together with the women and with Mary the mother of Jesus and with his brothers.

Acts 1.14

✝ Hail Mary ✝

The disciples went and preached everywhere.

Mark 16.20

✝ Hail Mary ✝

And the Lord worked with them and proved that their teaching was true by the miracles that were performed.

Mark 16.20

✝ Hail Mary ✝

Glory Be

THE THIRD GLORIOUS MYSTERY
The Descent of the Holy Spirit

Meditation

We remember that Jesus promised that he would never leave his friends alone. We call to mind that on Pentecost Jesus' followers were filled with the power of the Holy Spirit. Their hearts received God's peace and energy.

📖 **Our Father** 📖

"I will ask the Father, and he will give you another Helper, who will stay with you forever."
John 14.16

✝ **Hail Mary** ✝

"The Helper will come–the Spirit, who reveals the truth about God and who come from the Father. I will send him to you from the Father, and he will speak about me."
John 15.26

✝ **Hail Mary** ✝

When the day of Pentecost came,
all the believers were gathered
together in one place.

Acts 2.1

✝ **Hail Mary** ✝

Suddenly there was a noise from the sky
which sounded like a strong wind blowing,
and it filled the whole house
where they were sitting.

Acts 2.2

✝ **Hail Mary** ✝

Then they saw what looked like tongues of fire
which spread out and touched each person there.

Acts 2.3

✝ **Hail Mary** ✝

They were all filled with the Holy Spirit
and began to talk in other languages,
as the Spirit enabled them to speak.

Acts 2.4

✝ **Hail Mary** ✝

There were Jews living in Jerusalem,
religious people who had come
from every country of the world.
When they heard this noise,
a large crowd gathered.

Acts 2.5

✝ **Hail Mary** ✝

They were all excited because they heard the
believers talking in their own language…
Amazed and confused,
they kept asking each other,
"What does this mean?"

Acts 2.12

✝ **Hail Mary** ✝

Then Peter stood up with the
other eleven apostles
and in a loud voice began to say to the crowd:
"Fellow Jews and all of you who live in Jerusalem,
listen to me and let me tell you what this means."

Acts 2.14

✝ **Hail Mary** ✝

This is what the prophet Joel spoke about:
"This is what I will do in the last days,"
God says: "I will pour out my Spirit on everyone."
Acts 2.16

✝ **Hail Mary** ✝

Glory Be

THE FOURTH GLORIOUS MYSTERY
The Assumption of Mary into Heaven

Meditation

Just as Mary loved her son, so did Jesus have a very special love for his mother. Because of this special love, she was taken to heaven body and spirit. We can picture her in heaven with Jesus as she tells us how glorious heaven is. From heaven, Mary cares for us, as her children.

📖 Our Father 📖

Mary said: "My heart praises the Lord;"
Luke 1.46

✝ Hail Mary ✝

"my soul is glad because of God my Savior,"
Luke 1.47

✝ Hail Mary ✝

"for he has remembered me, his lowly servant."
Luke 1.47

✝ Hail Mary ✝

"From now on all people will call me happy,
because of the great things
the Mighty God has done for me."
Luke 1.49

✝ **Hail Mary** ✝

"His name is holy;
from one generation to another
he shows mercy to those who honor him."
Luke 1.50

✝ **Hail Mary** ✝

"He has stretched out his might arm
and scattered the proud with all their plans."
Luke 1.51

✝ **Hail Mary** ✝

"He has brought down mighty kings from their
thrones, and lifted up the lowly."
Luke 1.52

✝ **Hail Mary** ✝

"He has filled the hungry with good things, and sent the rich away with empty hands."

Luke 1.53

✝ **Hail Mary** ✝

"He has kept the promise he made to our ancestors, and has come to the help of his servant Israel."

Luke 1.54

✝ **Hail Mary** ✝

"He has remembered to show mercy to Abraham and to all his descendants forever!"

Luke 1.55

✝ **Hail Mary** ✝

Glory Be

THE FIFTH GLORIOUS MYSTERY
The Crowning of Mary
Queen of Heaven and Earth

Meditation

Not only does Jesus want his mother to be in heaven with Him but he prepares a special place for her. We imagine the angels and the holy souls around the throne of God, all of them glorifying God, as Jesus welcomes Mary to the center of heaven. He crowns her Queen of Heaven. She is now our Queen and the Queen of the Universe.

📖 **Our Father** 📖

After this I looked, and there was an enormous crowd – no one could count all the people.

Revelation 7.9

✝ **Hail Mary** ✝

They were there from every race, tribe, nation and language, and they stood in front of the throne and of the Lamb, dressed in white robes and held palm branches in their hands.

Revelation 7.9

✝ **Hail Mary** ✝

They called out in a loud voice "Salvation comes from our God, who sits on the throne and from the Lamb!"

Revelation 7.10

✝ **Hail Mary** ✝

Then a great and mysterious sight appeared in the sky. There was a woman, whose dress was the sun and who had the moon under her feet and a crown of twelve stars on her head."

Revelation 12.1

✝ **Hail Mary** ✝

Then I saw a new heaven and new earth… I saw the Holy City, the new Jerusalem, coming down out of heaven from God, prepared and ready, like a bride bring dressed to meet her husband.

Revelation 21.1,2

✝ **Hail Mary** ✝

I heard a loud voice speaking from the throne: "Now God's home is with people. He will live with them, and they shall be his people."

Revelation 21.3

✝ **Hail Mary** ✝

"God himself will be with them, and he will be their God."

Revelation 21.3

✝ Hail Mary ✝

"He will wipe away every tear from their eyes. There will be no more death, no more grief or crying or pain."

Revelation 21.4

✝ Hail Mary ✝

Then the one who sits upon the throne said, "And now I make all things new!"

Revelations 21.5

✝ Hail Mary ✝

"Listen!" says Jesus, "I am going soon! I will bring my rewards with me…"

Revelation 22.12

✝ Hail Mary ✝

Glory Be

Litany of the Blessed Virgin Mary

*L*ord, have mercy,

Christ, have mercy,

Lord, have mercy.

Christ, hear us.

Christ, graciously hear us.

God, the Father of heaven, have mercy on us.

God, the Son, Redeemer of the world,
    have mercy on us.

God, the Holy Spirit, have mercy on us.

Holy Trinity, one God, have mercy on us.

Holy Mary,

(after each invocation, respond with, "Pray for us")
                    -Pray for us.

Holy Mother of God,

Holy Virgin of virgins,

Mother of Christ,

Mother, full of grace,

Mother most pure,

Mother most chaste,

Immaculate Mother,

Sinless Mother,

Lovable Mother,

Model of mothers,

Mother of good counsel,

Mother of our Maker,

Mother of our Savior,

Wisest of virgins,

Holiest of virgins,

Virgin, powerful in the sight of God,

Virgin, merciful to us sinners,

Virgin, faithful to all God asks of you,

Mirror of holiness,

Seat of wisdom,

Cause of our joy,

Shrine of the Spirit,

Honor of your people,

Devoted handmaid of the Lord,

Mystical Rose,

Tower of David,

Tower of ivory,

House of gold,

Ark of the covenant,

Gate of heaven,